THE BEST
DOGS
EVER

BULLDOGS ARE THE BEST!

Elaine Landau

LERNER PUBLICATIONS COMPANY · MINNEAPOLIS

For Annemarie Roscello

Lerner Publications Company
A division of Lerner Publishing Group, Inc.
241 First Avenue North
Minneapolis, MN 55401 U.S.A.

Website address: www.lernerbooks.com

Library of Congress Cataloging-in-Publication Data

Landau, Elaine.
　　Bulldogs are the best! / by Elaine Landau.
　　　　p. cm. — (The best dogs ever)
　　Includes index.
　　ISBN 978-1-58013-566-5 (lib. bdg. : alk. paper)
　　1. Bulldog—Juvenile literature. I. Title.
　SF429.B85L36　2010
　636.72—dc22　　　　　　　　　2009020339

Manufactured in the United States of America
1 — BP — 12/15/09

TABLE OF CONTENTS

CHAPTER ONE
OH MY—IS THAT YOUR DOG?
4

CHAPTER TWO
WAY BACK WHEN
12

CHAPTER THREE
SHOULD A BULLDOG BE YOUR DOG?
18

CHAPTER FOUR
BRINGING YOUR BULLDOG HOME
24

Glossary 30   For More Information 31   Index 32

CHAPTER ONE

OH MY—IS THAT YOUR DOG?

Could you love a dog that looks unusual? What if people called your dog fat—or even ugly? Would you mind if someone said your dog looked like a tired old man?

Many bulldog owners have heard these things. But they strongly disagree with such views. They are proud of their pooches. They say that their dogs have rugged good looks.

A Rare and Special Beauty

Bulldog lovers don't mind their dog's wrinkles. Many think their pooch's sagging chin and loose skin are cute. Lots of people love this dog's waddling walk too.

Many people like the look of bulldogs. Bulldogs are one of the ten most popular dog breeds in the United States.

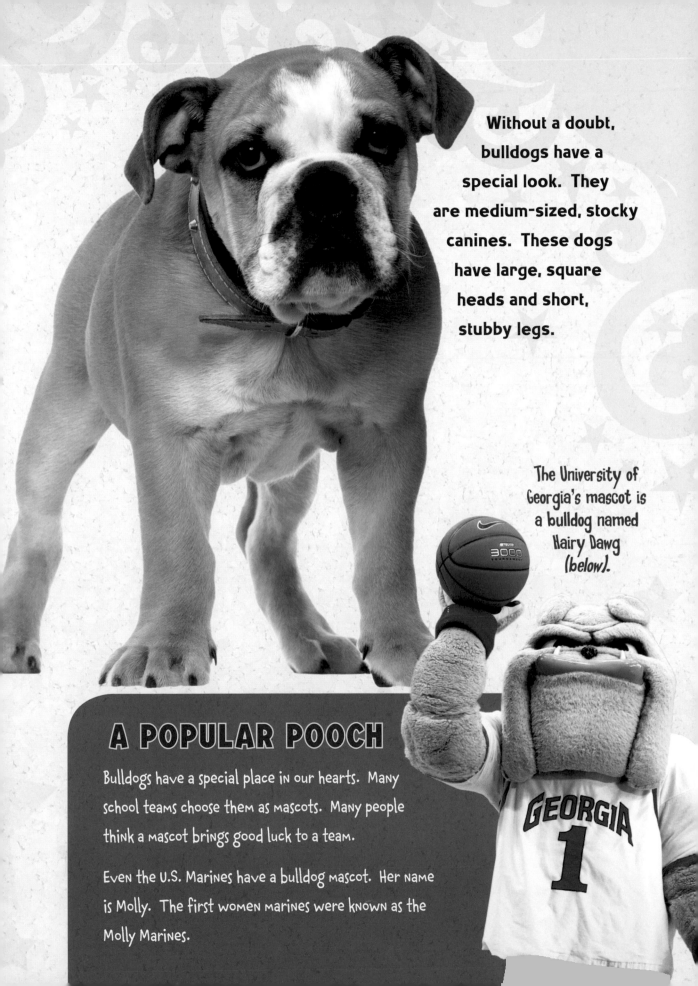

Without a doubt, bulldogs have a special look. They are medium-sized, stocky canines. These dogs have large, square heads and short, stubby legs.

The University of Georgia's mascot is a bulldog named Hairy Dawg (below).

A POPULAR POOCH

Bulldogs have a special place in our hearts. Many school teams choose them as mascots. Many people think a mascot brings good luck to a team.

Even the U.S. Marines have a bulldog mascot. Her name is Molly. The first women marines were known as the Molly Marines.

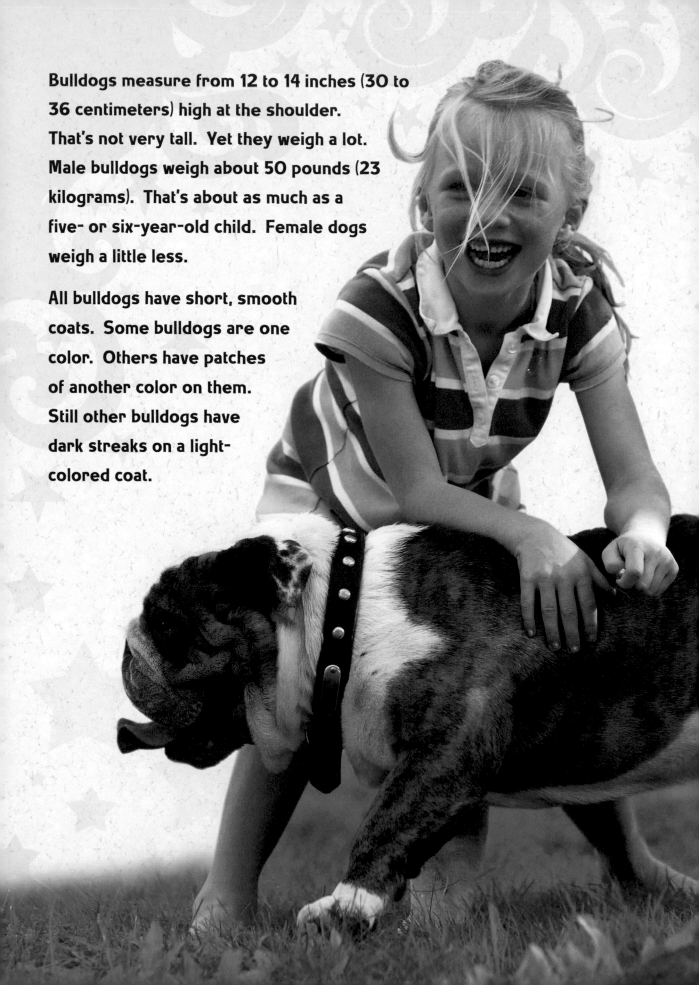

Bulldogs measure from 12 to 14 inches (30 to 36 centimeters) high at the shoulder. That's not very tall. Yet they weigh a lot. Male bulldogs weigh about 50 pounds (23 kilograms). That's about as much as a five- or six-year-old child. Female dogs weigh a little less.

All bulldogs have short, smooth coats. Some bulldogs are one color. Others have patches of another color on them. Still other bulldogs have dark streaks on a light-colored coat.

This bulldog has a solid color coat.

Some bulldogs, like the one above, have white patches on their fur. Others, like the one to the left, have dark streaks.

WHAT TO CALL YOUR WOOFER

A special dog needs a great name. Give your bulldog the best name you can think of. Do you like any of these?

VICTOR

Spike

PRINCESS

Blaze

Merlin

BOOMER

CHARMER

Duchess

Earl

Horace

A Classy Canine

Bulldog owners often brag about their pets' charm and style. These dogs have a calm, steady nature. They love people. And they are good with children and other animals.

Bulldogs want to be near their owners. They are quick to show their love too. Despite their weight, they still want to sit on your lap. They will also give you lots of big, wet kisses. Their owners think bulldogs are the best dogs ever.

CHAPTER TWO

WAY BACK WHEN

Modern-day bulldogs are sweet, loving pets. Yet that wasn't always true. These dogs have a dark past.

A Cruel Sport

The trouble began in England in the 1200s. People there used bulldogs for bullbaiting. Both a bull and a bulldog were needed for this sport. The dog tried to grab the bull's nose. Then it had to pull the bull to the ground. The bulls did not go down easily. They fought back hard. Their horns often tore the dog's flesh. Many bulldogs died in such fights.

This engraving of a bulldog was made in the early 1800s.

Those dogs were not like modern-day bulldogs. Back then, bulldogs had longer legs. They could easily reach a bull's nose. The sport was popular for hundreds of years. Finally, in 1835, the British government outlawed it. People could no longer use dogs to bait bulls.

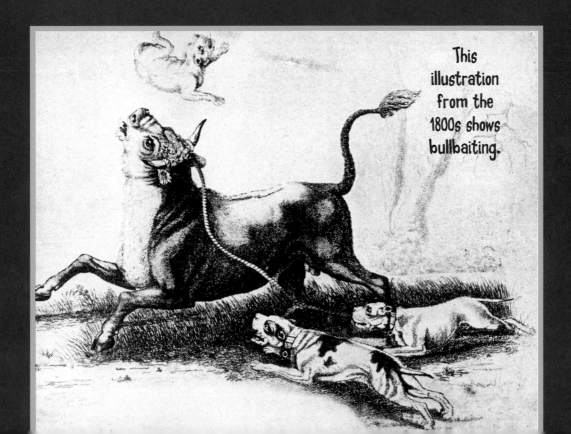

This illustration from the 1800s shows bullbaiting.

A new kind of bulldog was bred. This one looked very different from the early bulldogs. These canines were bred to be mild-mannered show dogs.

Bulldogs quickly became loving pets instead of fighting animals.

WEREN'T YOU IN A CARTOON?

A bulldog named Spike (below, left) has a role in the *Tom and Jerry* cartoon. Spike does not like cats. Yet he has a soft side. He's nice to mice. The dog is also very ticklish.

A Hit in the United States

Bulldogs became popular in the United States in the 1800s. Many were show dogs. But these dogs did more than just charm judges in the ring.

Lots of Americans fell for these special-looking dogs. People welcomed them into their homes. The bulldog became a much-loved pet.

WONDERFUL WINNERS

Bulldogs are winners. Two have won Best in Show at the Westminster Kennel Club Dog Show. A dog named Prince Albert took the prize in 1913. This princely pooch beat out a dozen other dogs that were also the best of their breeds.

In 1955, a bulldog called Kippax Fearnought won. Also known as Jack, this canine was known for his great walk.

These days, the American Kennel Club (AKC) groups dogs by breed. Some of the groups are the toy group, the sporting group, and the working group. The bulldog is in the nonsporting group.

This boxer belongs to the working group.

Springer spaniels, like this one, are in the sporting group.

Chihuahuas are in the toy group.

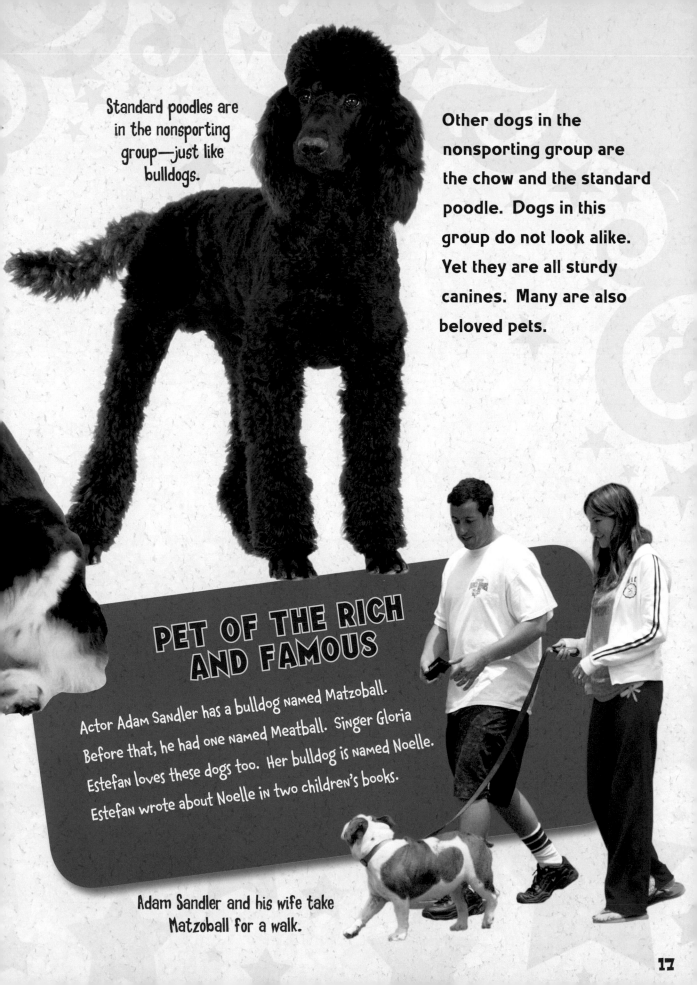

Standard poodles are in the nonsporting group—just like bulldogs.

Other dogs in the nonsporting group are the chow and the standard poodle. Dogs in this group do not look alike. Yet they are all sturdy canines. Many are also beloved pets.

PET OF THE RICH AND FAMOUS

Actor Adam Sandler has a bulldog named Matzoball. Before that, he had one named Meatball. Singer Gloria Estefan loves these dogs too. Her bulldog is named Noelle. Estefan wrote about Noelle in two children's books.

Adam Sandler and his wife take Matzoball for a walk.

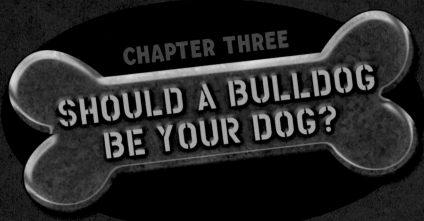

CHAPTER THREE

SHOULD A BULLDOG BE YOUR DOG?

Bulldogs are sturdy, sweet, and super loving. But is a bulldog the perfect pet for you? Read on to see.

Can You Spend Lots of Time with Your Pet?

Bulldogs love being with people. If left alone for too long, these dogs can behave badly. A bored bulldog may chew everything in sight.

Are you busy most days after school? Are you usually out of the house on weekends? Is anybody home during the day? Think about these things before getting a bulldog.

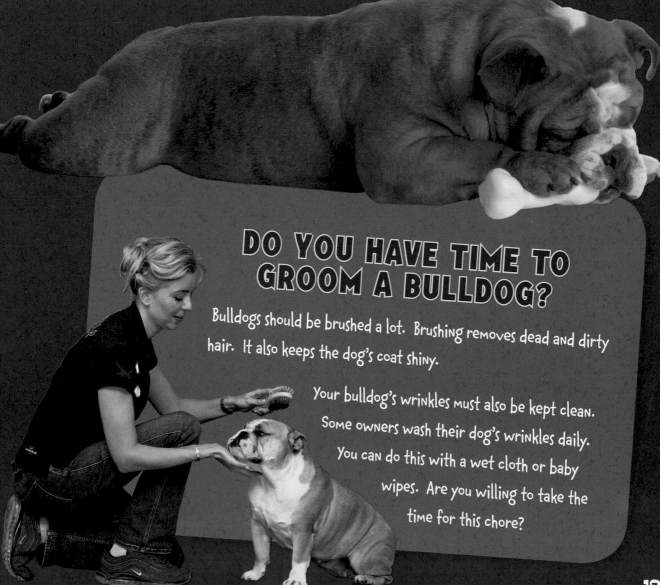

DO YOU HAVE TIME TO GROOM A BULLDOG?

Bulldogs should be brushed a lot. Brushing removes dead and dirty hair. It also keeps the dog's coat shiny.

Your bulldog's wrinkles must also be kept clean. Some owners wash their dog's wrinkles daily. You can do this with a wet cloth or baby wipes. Are you willing to take the time for this chore?

Do You Live in a Cool Place?

Bulldogs are cool pets. They also have to be kept cool. These dogs cannot stand the heat. Some bulldogs have even died from heatstroke. Can you always keep your house at about 70°F (21°C)? That may mean keeping the air conditioner on a lot. Be sure your family is willing to do this.

Bulldogs pant to cool themselves down.

IS THAT SNORING I HEAR?

Bulldogs have short snouts. Their snouts even look as if they're pushed in. Dogs with short snouts tend to breathe heavily. And when they breathe, they make a lot of noise.

Some bulldogs snore when they are sleeping. Would a snoring canine drive you crazy? If so, you might want to pick another pet.

Are You Very Active?

Do you enjoy running and jogging? Do you like outdoor sports? If so, don't plan to do these things with your bulldog. Bulldogs are true couch potatoes. These dogs are hardly exercise hounds. They are happy just to snooze on your lap or rest at your feet.

Do You Need a Watchdog?

Are you looking for a dog that will protect your home? If so, pick a different canine. Bulldogs like meeting new people. Don't count on your bulldog to attack a robber. It might be thrilled to have some company.

Bulldogs may look fierce and unwelcoming, but they are really eager to meet new people.

DID YOUR DOG PASS GAS?

Bulldogs pass a lot of gas. You can tell by the smell. There isn't much you can do about it. If it happens in the car, open the window a bit. You need a sense of humor to have a bulldog.

CHAPTER FOUR

BRINGING YOUR BULLDOG HOME

The big day is here! You're about to bring your new pooch home. Maybe you have a camera ready. Photos are great. But you'll need a lot more.

Buy the Basics

Be ready to care for your pet. Have your dog supplies before you get your dog. Here's a short list of what you'll need:

- collar
- leash
- tags (for identification)
- dog food
- food and water bowls
- crates (one for when your pet travels by car and one for it to rest in at home)
- treats (to be used in training)
- toys

IT'S PLAYTIME!

Don't let your bulldog get bored. Get your pooch some fun playthings. Your bulldog may like these toys:

- nylon bones to chew on
- squeaky toys (that are too large for your dog to swallow)
- thick ropelike toys for playing tug

Off to the Doggie Doctor

You'll also want to take your dog to a veterinarian soon.
Veterinarians, or vets, are doctors who care for animals.
The vet will give your bulldog shots. This is important for its
health. Your dog will need to go back to the vet for checkups.
And be sure to take your dog to the vet if it gets sick.

Feeding Fido

Your bulldog needs a healthful diet. Dog food comes in many forms. There are dry dog foods and canned, wet foods. You can also get frozen food for your dog. A 50-pound (23 kg) bulldog needs about 1 pound (0.5 kg) of food a day. Ask your vet which food is best for your dog.

Have Fun with Your Dog

Make your bulldog your best buddy. Bulldogs are not built for lots of exercise. But they do like to have fun. Bulldogs will happily chase tennis balls around the house. They'll go for short walks with you too. Some bulldogs have even learned to skateboard.

TRAINING TIME

Start training your dog right away. Be patient and loving with your pet. Bulldogs are not always easy to train. They have minds of their own. Yet in time, they'll learn the basics.

Your bulldog will be a loyal friend. It will also be a great, goofy pal. You can count on this special dog to bring you miles of smiles.

GLOSSARY

American Kennel Club (AKC): an organization that groups dogs by breed. The AKC also defines the characteristics of different breeds.

breed: a particular type of dog. Dogs of the same breed have the same body shape and general features. *Breed* can also refer to producing puppies.

canine: a dog, or having to do with dogs

coat: a dog's fur

diet: the food your dog eats

groom: to clean, brush, and trim a dog's coat

heatstroke: a dangerous condition caused by being exposed to too much heat

mascot: a person, animal, or thing chosen by a group to bring luck to the team it represents

nonsporting group: a group of many different types of dogs that are squarely built and sturdy. Dogs in the nonsporting group generally lack the characteristics of hunting dogs.

snout: the front part of a dog's head. It includes the nose, mouth, and jaws.

veterinarian: a doctor who treats animals. Veterinarians are called vets for short.

FOR MORE INFORMATION

Books

Brecke, Nicole, and Patricia M. Stockland. *Dogs You Can Draw*. Minneapolis: Millbrook Press, 2010. This colorful book teaches readers how to draw different kinds of dogs and shares fun facts about each breed.

Gray, Susan H. *Bulldogs*. Mankato, MN: Child's World, 2008. Read this fun book to learn more about bulldogs.

Landau, Elaine. *Your Pet Dog*. Rev. ed. New York: Children's Press, 2007. This title is a good guide for young people on choosing and caring for a dog.

Stone, Lynn M. *Bulldogs*. Vero Beach, FL: Rourke Publishing, 2007. Read all about the bulldog's characteristics and history in this book.

Websites

American Kennel Club
http://www.akc.org
Visit this website to find a complete listing of AKC-registered dog breeds, including the bulldog. The site also has fun printable activities for kids.

ASPCA Animaland
http://www2.aspca.org/site/PageServer?pagename=kids_pc _home
Check out this page for helpful hints on caring for a dog and other pets.

Index

American Kennel Club
(AKC), 16

coat, 8, 19
color, 8

exercise, 21, 28

food, 25, 27

grooming, 19

health, 20, 26-27
history, 12-15

mascot, 7

names, 10
nonsporting group, 16-17

size, 7-8

training, 25, 28

Westminster Kennel Club
Dog Show, 15

Photo Acknowledgments

The images in this book are used with the permission of: backgrounds © iStockphoto.com/Julie Fisher and © iStockphoto.com/Tomasz Adamczyk; © iStockphoto.com/Michael Balderas, p. 1; © Annette Shaff/Dreamstime.com, p. 4; © Mistik Pictures/Photographer's Choice/Getty Images, p. 5; © Tammy Mcallister/Dreamstime.com, pp. 6 (left), 25 (top); © Image Source/Getty Images, p. 6 (right); © Eric Isselée/Dreamstime.com, p. 7 (top); © Darrell Walker/Icon SMI/ZUMA Press, p. 7 (bottom); © Cusp/SuperStock, pp. 8-9; © iStockphoto.com/John Burwell, BurwellPhotography.com, p. 9 (top); © Jackieblue/Dreamstime.com, p. 9 (bottom); © Sean Murphy/Stone+/Getty Images, p. 10; © Yellow Dog Productions/Riser/Getty Images, p. 11; © Sharon Montrose/Digital Vision/Getty Images, p. 12; © Mary Evans/Photo Researchers, Inc., p. 13 (top); Mary Evans Picture Library/Everett Collection, p. 13 (bottom); © Buyenlarge/Hulton Archvie/Getty Images, p. 14 (top); © Photofest, p. 14 (bottom); © Topical Press Agency/Hulton Archive/Getty Images, p. 15; © Jerry Shulman/SuperStock, p. 16 (left); © GK Hart/Vikki Hart/Photodisc/Getty Images, p. 16 (top right); © Andrey Medvedev/Dreamstime.com, p. 16 (bottom right); © iStockphoto.com/Eric Isselée, p. 17 (top); © 266/Most Wanted/ZUMA Press, p. 17 (bottom); © Willeecole/Dreamstime.com, pp. 18, 19 (top); © blickwinkel/Alamy, p. 19 (bottom); © Susan Leggett/Dreamstime.com, p. 20; © LWA/Photographer's Choice/Getty Images, p. 21; © Ben Molyneux Dogs/Alamy, p. 22 (top); © Flirt/SuperStock, pp. 22 (bottom), 27; © Blake Little/The Image Bank/Getty Images, p. 23; © Jane Burton/Photo Researchers, Inc., p. 24; © Yves Lanceau/NHPA/Photoshot, pp. 24-25; © April Turner/Dreamstime.com, p. 25 (center); © iStockphoto.com/orix3, p. 25 (bottom); © LWA/Larry Williams/Blend Images/Getty Images, p. 26; © Nikki O'Keefe Images/Flickr/Getty Images, pp. 28-29; © LWA/Photodisc/Getty Images, p. 28; © Tanya Constantine/UpperCut Images/Getty Images, p. 29.

Front Cover: © Jeffrey Coolidge/The Image Bank/Getty Images.
Back Cover: © Mistik Pictures/Photographer's Choice/Getty Images.